BEYOND THE
PLEASURE
PRINCIPLE

BEYOND THE PLEASURE PRINCIPLE

SIGMUND FREUD

pac ps

Pacific Publishing Studio

Cover Photography: S&A Alfano, M Stroz

Translation: James Strachey

CONTENTS

Chapter One
1

Chapter Two
11

Chapter Three
21

Chapter Four
35

Chapter Five
55

Chapter Six
73

Chapter Seven
107

Chapter One

In the theory of psychoanalysis, we have no hesitation in assuming that the course taken by mental events is automatically regulated by the pleasure principle. We believe, that is to say, that the course of those events is invariably set in motion by an unpleasurable tension; and that it takes a direction such that its final outcome coincides with a lowering of that tension—that is, with an avoidance of unpleasure or a production of pleasure.

In taking that course into account, in our consideration of the mental processes that are the subject of our study, we are introducing an economic point of view into our work. If, in describing those processes, we try to estimate this economic factor in addition to the topographical and dynamic ones, we shall, I think, be giving the most complete description of them we can presently conceive, and one that deserves to be distinguished by the term meta-psychological.

It is of no concern to us, in this connection, to enquire how far—with this hypothesis of the pleasure principle—we have approached or adopted any particular, historically established, philosophical system. We have arrived at these speculative assumptions in an attempt to describe and to account for the facts of daily observation in our field of study.

Priority and originality are not among the aims that psycho-analytic work sets itself; and the impressions that underlie the hypothesis of the pleasure principle are so obvious that they can scarcely be overlooked. On the other hand, we would readily express our gratitude to any philosophical or psychological theory that was able to inform us of the meaning of the feelings of pleasure and unpleasure, which act so imperatively upon us.

However, on this point we are, alas, offered nothing to our purpose. This is the most obscure and inaccessible region of the mind, and, because we cannot avoid contact with it, the least rigid hypothesis, it seems to me, will be the best.

We have decided to relate pleasure and unpleasure to the quantity of excitation that is present in the mind but is not in any way bound; and to relate them in such a manner that unpleasure corresponds to an *increase* in the quantity of excitation and pleasure to a *diminution*.

What we are implying is not a simple relation between the strength of the feelings of pleasure and unpleasure, and the corresponding modifications in the quantity of excitation; least of all—in view of all we have been taught by psychophysiology—are we suggesting any directly proportional ratio. The factor that determines the feeling is probably the amount of increase or diminution in the quantity of excitation *in a given period of time.*

Experiment might possibly play a part here; but it is not advisable for analysts to go into the problem further, so long as our way is not pointed by quite definite observations.

We cannot, however, remain indifferent to the discovery that an investigator of such penetration as G. T. Fechner held a view upon the subject of pleasure and unpleasure that coincides in all essentials with the one that has been forced upon us by psycho-analytic work.

Fechner's statement is to be found contained in a small work, *Einige Ideen zur Schöpfungs,* and reads as follows:

"In so far as conscious impulses always have some relation to pleasure or unpleasure, pleasure and unpleasure, too, can be regarded as having a psycho-physical relation to conditions of stability and instability. This provides a basis for a hypothesis into which I propose to enter in greater detail elsewhere. According to this hypothesis, every psycho-physical movement crossing the threshold of consciousness is attended by pleasure in proportion as, beyond a certain limit, it approximates to complete stability, and is attended by unpleasure in proportion as, beyond a certain limit, it deviates from complete stability. While between the two limits, which may be described as qualitative thresholds of pleasure and unpleasure, there is a certain margin of aesthetic indifference..."

The facts that have caused us to believe in the dominance of the pleasure principle in mental life also find expression in the hypothesis that the mental apparatus endeavors to keep the quantity of excitation present in it as low as possible, or at least to keep it constant.

This latter hypothesis is only another way of stating the pleasure principle. For if the work of the mental apparatus is directed toward keeping the quantity of excitation low, then anything calculated to increase that quantity is bound to be felt as adverse to the functioning of the apparatus, that is, as unpleasurable.

The pleasure principle follows from the constancy principle. Moreover, a more detailed discussion will show that the tendency, which we thus attribute to the mental apparatus, is subsumed as a special case under Fechner's principle of the *tendency towards stability*, to which he has brought the feelings of pleasure and unpleasure into relation.

It must be pointed out, however, that strictly speaking it is incorrect to talk of the dominance of the pleasure principle over the course of mental processes. If such a dominance existed, the immense majority of our mental processes would have to be accompanied by pleasure or to lead to pleasure, whereas universal experience completely contradicts any such conclusion. The most that can be said, therefore, is that there exists, in the mind, a strong *tendency* toward the pleasure principle, but that tendency is opposed by certain other forces or circumstances, so that the final outcome cannot always be in harmony with the tendency toward pleasure.

We may compare what Fechner remarks on a similar point: "Because tendency toward an aim does not imply that the aim is attained, and because, in general, the aim is attainable only by approximations..."

If we turn now to the question of what circumstances are able to prevent the pleasure principle from being carried into effect, we find ourselves once more on secure and well-trodden ground. In framing our answer, we have at our disposal a rich fund of analytic experience.

The first example of the pleasure principle being inhibited in this way is a familiar one, which occurs with regularity. We know that the pleasure principle is proper to a *primary* method of working on the part of the mental apparatus, but that, from the point of view of the self-preservation of the organism among the difficulties of the external world, it is from the very outset inefficient and even highly dangerous.

Under the influence of the ego's instincts of self-preservation, the pleasure principle is replaced by the *reality principle*. This latter principle does not abandon the intention of ultimately obtaining pleasure, but it nevertheless demands and carries into effect the postponement of satisfaction, the abandonment of a number of possibilities of gaining satisfaction, and the temporary toleration of unpleasure, as a step on the long indirect road to pleasure.

The pleasure principle long persists, however, as the method of working, employed by the sexual instincts, which are so hard to educate, and, starting out from those instincts, or in the ego itself, it often succeeds in overcoming the reality principle, to the detriment of the organism as a whole.

There can be no doubt, however, that the replacement of the pleasure principle by the reality principle can only be made responsible for a small number, and by no means the most intense of unpleasurable experiences. Another occasion of the release of unpleasure, which occurs with no less regularity, is to be found in the conflicts and dissensions that take place in the mental apparatus while the ego is passing through its development into more highly composite organizations.

Almost all the energy, with which the apparatus is filled, arises from its innate instinctual impulses. These are not all allowed to reach the same phases of development. In the course of development, it happens again and again that individual instincts or parts of instincts turn out to be incompatible in their aims or demands with the remaining ones, which are able to combine into the inclusive unity of the ego.

The former are then split off from this unity by the process of repression, held back at lower levels of psychical development and cut off, to begin with, from the possibility of satisfaction. If they succeed subsequently, as can so easily happen with repressed sexual instincts, in struggling through, by roundabout paths, to a direct or to a substitutive satisfaction, that event, which would in other cases have been an opportunity for pleasure, is felt by the ego as unpleasure.

Consequently, of the old conflict which ended in repression, a new breach has occurred in the pleasure principle at the very time when certain instincts were endeavoring, in accordance with the principle, to obtain fresh pleasure.

The details of the process by which repression turns a possibility of pleasure into a source of unpleasure are not yet clearly understood or cannot be clearly represented. However, there is no doubt that all neurotic unpleasure is of that kind— pleasure that cannot be felt as such.

The two sources of unpleasure, which I have just indicated, are very far from covering the majority of our unpleasurable experiences. As regards the remainder, it can be asserted, with some show of justification, that their presence does not contradict the dominance of the pleasure principle. Most of the unpleasure that we experience is *perceptual* unpleasure. It is either perception of pressure by unsatisfied instincts, or external perception that is either distressing in itself, or that which excites unpleasurable expectations in the mental apparatus, that is, which is recognized by it as a danger.

The reaction to these instinctual demands and threats of danger, a reaction that constitutes the proper activity of the mental apparatus, can then be directed in a correct manner by the pleasure principle or the modified reality principle. This does not seem to necessitate any far-reaching limitation of the pleasure principle.

Nevertheless, the investigation of the mental reaction to external danger is precisely a subject that may produce new material and raise fresh questions bearing upon our present problem.

Chapter Two

A condition has long been known and described which occurs after severe mechanical concussions, railway disasters, and other accidents involving a risk to life. It has been given the name, traumatic neurosis. The terrible war, which has just ended, gave rise to a great number of illnesses of this kind, but it at least put an end to the temptation to attribute the cause of the disorder to organic lesions of the nervous system, brought about by mechanical force.

The symptomatic picture presented by traumatic neurosis approaches that of hysteria in the wealth of its similar motor symptoms, but surpasses it, as a rule, in its strongly marked signs of subjective ailment (in which it resembles hypochondria or melancholia), as well as in the evidence it gives of a far more comprehensive general enfeeblement and disturbance of the mental capacities.

No complete explanation has yet been reached either of war neuroses or of the traumatic neuroses of peace. In the case of the war neuroses, the fact that the same symptoms sometimes came about without the intervention of any gross mechanical violence, seemed at once enlightening and bewildering.

In the case of the ordinary traumatic neuroses, two characteristics emerge prominently. First, that the chief weight in their causation seems to rest upon the factor of surprise, of fright; and secondly, that a wound or injury inflicted simultaneously works, as a rule, *against* the development of a neurosis.

Fright, fear, and anxiety are improperly used as synonymous expressions; they are, in fact, capable of clear distinction in their relation to danger. Anxiety describes a particular state of expecting the danger or preparing for it, even though it may be an unknown one. Fear requires a definite object of which to be afraid. Fright, however, is the name we give to the state a person gets into when he has run into danger without being prepared for it. It emphasizes the factor of surprise.

I do not believe anxiety can produce a traumatic neurosis. There is something about anxiety that protects its subject against fright and so against fright-neuroses. We shall return to this point later.

The study of dreams may be considered the most trustworthy method of investigating deep mental processes. Now, dreams occurring in traumatic neuroses have the characteristic of repeatedly bringing the patient back into the situation of his accident, a situation from which he wakes up in another fright. This astonishes people far too little. They think the fact that the traumatic experience is constantly forcing itself upon the patient even in his sleep is a proof of the strength of that experience. The patient is, as one might say, fixated to his trauma.

Fixations to the experience that started the illness have long been familiar to us in hysteria. Hysterics are, to a great extent, suffering from reminiscences. In the war neuroses, too, observers like Ferenczi and Simmel have been able to explain certain motor symptoms by fixation to the moment at which the trauma occurred.

I am not aware, however, that patients suffering from traumatic neurosis are much occupied in their waking lives with memories of their accident.

Perhaps, they are more concerned with not thinking of it. Anyone who accepts it as something self-evident that their dreams should put them back at night into the situation that caused them to fall ill has misunderstood the nature of dreams.

It would be more in harmony with their nature to show the patient pictures from his healthy past, or of the cure for which he hopes. If we are not to be shaken in our belief in the wish-fulfilling tenor of dreams by the dreams of traumatic neurotics, we still have one resource open to us: we may argue that the function of dreaming, like so much else, is upset in this condition and diverted from its purposes, or we may be driven to reflect on the mysterious masochistic trends of the ego.

At this point, I propose to leave the dark and dismal subject of the traumatic neurosis and pass on to examine the method of working employed by the mental apparatus in one of its earliest *normal* activities—I mean in children's play.

The different theories of children's play have only recently been summarized and discussed from the psycho-analytic point of view by Pfeifer (1919), to whose paper I would refer my readers. These theories attempt to discover the motives that lead children to play, but they fail to bring into the foreground the *economic* motive—the consideration of the yield of pleasure involved.

Without wishing to include the whole field covered by these phenomena, I have been able, through a chance opportunity that presented itself, to throw some light upon the first game played by a little boy of one and a half and invented by himself.

It was more than a mere fleeting observation, for I lived under the same roof as the child and his parents for some weeks, and it was some time before I discovered the meaning of the puzzling activity, which he constantly repeated.

The child was not at all precocious in his intellectual development. At the age of one and a half, he could say only a few comprehensible words. He could also make use of a number of sounds, which expressed a meaning intelligible to those around him. He was, however, on good terms with his parents and their one servant-girl, and tributes were paid to his being a good boy.

He did not disturb his parents at night; he conscientiously obeyed orders not to touch certain things or go into certain rooms, and above all he never cried when his mother left him for a few hours. At the same time, he was greatly attached to his mother, who had not only fed him herself but had also looked after him without any outside help.

This good little boy, however, had an occasional disturbing habit of taking any small objects he could get hold of and throwing them away from himself, into a corner, under the bed, and so on, so that hunting for his toys and picking them up was often quite a business. As he did this, he gave vent to a loud, long-drawn-out "o-o-o-o," accompanied by an expression of interest and satisfaction.

His mother, and the writer of the present account, were agreed in thinking that this was not a mere interjection but represented the German word for "gone". I eventually realized that it was a game and that the only use he made of any of his toys was to play *gone* with them.

One day, I made an observation that confirmed my view. The child had a wooden reel with a piece of string tied around it. It never occurred to him to pull it along the floor behind him, for instance, and play at its being a carriage. What he did was to hold the reel by the string and, very skillfully, throw it over the edge of his curtained cot, so that it disappeared into it, at the same time uttering his expressive "o-o-o-o."

He then pulled the reel out of the cot again by the string and hailed its reappearance with a joyful "da" ("there"). This, then, was the complete game—disappearance and return. As a rule, one only witnessed its first act, which was repeated untiringly as a game in itself, though there is no doubt that greater pleasure was attached to the second act.

The interpretation of the game then became obvious. It was related to the child's great cultural achievement—the instinctual renunciation (that is, the renunciation of instinctual satisfaction) which he had made in allowing his mother to go away without protesting. He compensated himself for this, as it were, by himself staging the disappearance and return of the objects within his reach.

It is, of course, a matter of indifference from the point of view of judging the affective nature of the game, whether the child invented it himself or took it over on some outside suggestion. Our interest is directed to another point. The child cannot possibly have felt his mother's departure as something agreeable or even indifferent. How then does his repetition of this distressing experience as a game fit in with the pleasure principle?

It may, perhaps, be said in reply that her departure had to be enacted as a necessary preliminary to her joyful return, and that it was in the latter that lay the true purpose of the game. But against this must be counted the observed fact that the first act, that of the departure, was staged as a game, in itself, and far more frequently than the episode in its entirety with its pleasurable ending.

A further observation subsequently confirmed this interpretation fully. One day, the child's mother had been away for several hours and on her return was met with the words, "Baby, o-o-o-o!" which was at first incomprehensible. It soon turned out, however, that during this long period of solitude, the child had found a method of making *himself* disappear. He had discovered his reflection in a full-length mirror, which did not quite reach to the ground, so that by crouching down he could make his mirror-image "gone."

No certain decision can be reached from the analysis of a single case like this. On an unprejudiced view, one gets an impression that the child turned his experience into a game from another motive. At the outset, he was in a *passive* situation. He was overpowered by the experience;

but, by repeating it, unpleasurable though it was, as a game, he took on an *active* part.

These efforts might be put down to an instinct for mastery, acting independently of whether the repeated memory was, in itself, pleasurable or not. But still, another interpretation may be attempted. Throwing away the object so that it was "gone," might satisfy an impulse of the child's, which was suppressed in his actual life, to revenge himself on his mother for going away from him.

In that case, it would have a defiant meaning: "All right, then, go away! I don't need you. I'm sending you away myself."

A year later, the same boy, whom I had observed at his first game, used to take a toy if he was angry with it, and throw it on the floor, exclaiming: "Go to the fwont!" He had heard, at that time, that his absent father was "at the front," and was far from regretting his absence. On the contrary, he made it quite clear that he had no desire to be disturbed in his sole possession of his mother.

We know of other children who like to express similar hostile impulses by throwing away objects instead of persons. We are, therefore, left in doubt as to whether the impulse to work over in the mind some overpowering experience, so as to make oneself master of it can find expression as a primary event, and independently of the pleasure principle.

For, in the case we have been discussing, the child may, after all, only have been able to repeat his unpleasant experience in play because the repetition carried, along with it, a yield of pleasure of another sort, but none the less a direct one.

Nor shall we be helped in our hesitation between these two views by further considering children's play. It is clear that in their play, children repeat everything that has made a great impression on them in real life, and that in so doing they abreact the strength of the impression and, as one might put it, make themselves master of the situation.

But on the other hand, it is obvious that all their play is influenced by a wish that dominates them the whole time—the wish to be grown-up and to be able to do what grown-up people do. It can also be observed that the unpleasurable nature of an experience does not always un-suit it for play. If the doctor looks down a child's throat, or carries out some small operation on him, we may be quite sure that these frightening experiences will be the subject of the next game; but we must not, in that connection, overlook the fact that there is a yield of pleasure from another source.

As the child passes over from the passivity of the experience to the activity of the game, he hands on the disagreeable experience to one of his playmates, and in this way revenges himself on a substitute.

Nevertheless, it emerges from this discussion that there is no need to assume the existence of a special imitative instinct in order to provide a motive for play. Finally, a reminder may be added that the artistic play and artistic imitation carried out by adults, which, unlike children's, are aimed at an audience, do not spare the spectators (in tragedy, for instance) the most painful experiences, and can yet, be felt by them as highly enjoyable.

This is convincing proof that, even under the dominance of the pleasure principle, there are ways and means enough of making what is in itself unpleasurable into a subject to be recollected and worked over in the mind.

The consideration of these cases and situations, which have a yield of pleasure as their final outcome, should be undertaken by some system of aesthetics with an economic approach to its subject-matter. They are of no use for our purposes, because they presuppose the existence and dominance of the pleasure principle. They give no evidence of the operation of tendencies *beyond* the pleasure principle, that is, of tendencies more primitive than it and independent of it.

Chapter Three

Twenty-five years of intense work have had, as their result, that the immediate aims of psychoanalytic technique are quite other today than they were at the outset. At first, the analyzing physician could do no more than discover the unconscious material that was concealed from the patient, put it together, and, at the right moment, communicate it to him.

Psychoanalysis was then, first and foremost, an art of interpreting. Because this did not solve the therapeutic problem, a further aim quickly came in view: to oblige the patient to confirm the analyst's construction from his own memory. In that endeavor, the chief emphasis lay upon the patient's resistances: the art consisted now in uncovering these as quickly as possible, in pointing them out to the patient, and in inducing him by human influence. This was where suggestion, operating as transference, played its part to abandon his resistances.

But it became ever clearer that the aim which had been set up—namely, that what was unconscious should become conscious—is not completely attainable by that method. The patient cannot remember the whole of what is repressed in him, and what he cannot remember may be precisely the essential part of it. Thus, he acquires no sense of conviction of the correctness of the construction that has been communicated to him.

He is obliged to *repeat* the repressed material as a contemporary experience instead of, as the physician would prefer to see, *remembering* it as something belonging to the past. These reproductions, which emerge with such unwished-for exactitude, always have, as their subject, some portion of infantile sexual life—of the Oedipus complex, that is, and its derivatives.

They are invariably played out in the sphere of the transference, of the patient's relation to the physician. When things have reached this stage, it may be said that the earlier neurosis has now been replaced by a fresh, transference neurosis. It has been the physician's endeavor to keep this transference neurosis within the narrowest limits:

to force as much as possible into the channel of memory and to allow as little as possible to emerge as repetition.

The ratio between what is remembered and what is reproduced varies from case to case. The physician cannot, as a rule, spare his patient this phase of the treatment. He must get him to re-experience some portion of his forgotten life, but must see to it, on the other hand, that the patient retains some degree of aloofness, which will enable him, in spite of everything, to recognize that what appears to be reality is, in fact, only a reflection of a forgotten past.

If this can be successfully achieved, the patient's sense of conviction is won, together with the therapeutic success that is dependent on it.

In order to make it easier to understand this compulsion to repeat, which emerges during the psycho-analytic treatment of neurotics, we must above all get rid of the mistaken notion that what we are dealing with, in our struggle against resistances, is resistance on the part of the unconscious.

The unconscious—that is to say, the repressed—offers no resistance whatever to the efforts of the treatment. Indeed, it itself has no other endeavor than to break through the pressure weighing down on it and force its way either into consciousness or to discharge through some real action.

Resistance during treatment arises from the same higher strata and systems of the mind, which originally carried out repression. But the fact that, as we know from experience, the motives of the resistances, and indeed the resistances themselves, are unconscious at first during the treatment, is a hint to us that we should correct a shortcoming in our terminology. We shall avoid a lack of clarity if we make our contrast, not between the conscious and the unconscious, but between the coherent ego and the repressed.

It is certain that much of the ego is itself unconscious, and notably, what we may describe as its nucleus. Only a small part of it is covered by the term preconscious. Having replaced a purely descriptive terminology by one that is systematic or dynamic, we can say that the patient's resistance arises from his ego, and we then, at once, perceive that the compulsion to repeat must be ascribed to the unconscious repressed. It seems probable that that compulsion can only express itself after the work of treatment has gone half-way to meet it, and has loosened the repression.

There is no doubt that the resistance of the conscious and unconscious ego operates under the sway of the pleasure principle. It seeks to avoid the unpleasure, which would be produced by the liberation of the repressed. Our efforts, on the other hand, are directed toward procuring the toleration of that unpleasure by an appeal to the reality principle. But how is the compulsion to repeat—the manifestation of the power of the repressed—related to the pleasure principle?

It is clear that the greater part of what is re-experienced under the compulsion to repeat must cause the ego unpleasure, because it brings to light activities of repressed instinctual impulses. That, however, is unpleasure of a kind we have already considered and does not contradict the pleasure principle: unpleasure for one system and simultaneously satisfaction for the other.

But we come, now, to a new and remarkable fact, namely that the compulsion to repeat also recalls from the past experiences, which include no possibility of pleasure, and which can never, even long ago, have brought satisfaction even to instinctual impulses that have since been repressed.

The early efflorescence of infantile sexual life is doomed to come to an end because its wishes are incompatible with reality and with the inadequate stage of development that the child has reached. That efflorescence perishes in the most distressing circumstances and to the accompaniment of the most painful feelings. Loss of love and failure leave behind them a permanent injury to self-assurance in the form of a narcissistic scar, which in my opinion, as well as in Marcinowski's (1918), contributes more than anything to the sense of inferiority that is so common in neurotics.

Sexual researches, on which limits are imposed by a child's physical development, lead to no satisfactory conclusion; hence such later complaints as "I can't accomplish anything; I can't succeed in anything."

The tie of affection, which binds the child as a rule to the parent of the opposite sex, succumbs to disappointment, to a vain expectation of satisfaction, or to jealousy over the birth of a new baby—unmistakable proof of the infidelity of the object of the child's affections. His own attempt to make a baby himself, carried out with tragic seriousness, fails shamefully. The lessening amount of affection he receives, the increasing demands of education, hard words, and an occasional punishment—these show him at last the full extent to which he has been scorned. These are a few typical and constantly recurring instances of the ways in which the love characteristic of the age of childhood is brought to an end.

Patients repeat all of these unwanted situations and painful emotions in the transference, and revive them with the greatest ingenuity. They seek to bring about the interruption of the treatment while it is still incomplete; they contrive once more to feel themselves scorned, to oblige the physician to speak severely to them, and treat them coldly.

They discover appropriate objects for their jealousy; instead of the passionately desired baby of their childhood, they produce a plan or a promise of some grand present—which turns out, as a rule, to be no less unreal.

None of these things can have produced pleasure in the past; and it might be supposed that they would cause less unpleasure today if they emerged as memories or dreams rather than taking the form of fresh experiences. They are, of course, the activities of instincts intended to lead to satisfaction; but no lesson has been learned from the old experience of these activities, having led instead only to unpleasure. In spite of that, they are repeated, under pressure of a compulsion.

What psychoanalysis reveals in the transference phenomena of neurotics can also be observed in the lives of some normal people. The impression they give is of being pursued by a malignant fate or possessed by some extraneous power; but psychoanalysis has always taken the view that their fate is, for the most part, arranged by themselves and determined by early infantile influences. The compulsion, which is here in evidence, differs in no way from the compulsion to repeat—which we have found in neurotics, even though the people we are now considering have never shown any signs of dealing with a neurotic conflict by producing symptoms.

Thus we have come across people all of whose human relationships have the same outcome: such as the benefactor who is abandoned in anger after a time by each of his *protégés*, however much they may otherwise differ from one another, and who thus seems doomed to taste all the bitterness of ingratitude; or the man whose friendships all end in betrayal by his friend; or the man who, time after time, in the course of his life raises someone else into a position of great private or public authority and then, after a certain interval, himself upsets that authority and replaces him by a new one; or, again, the lover each of whose love affairs with a woman passes through the same phases and reaches the same conclusion.

This *ewige Wiederkehr des Gleichen* causes us no astonishment when it relates to active behavior on the part of the person concerned, and when we can discern in him an essential character-trait, which always remains the same, and which is compelled to find expression in a repetition of the same experiences.

We are much more impressed by cases where the subject appears to have a passive experience, over which he has no influence, but in which he meets with a repetition of the same fatality. There is the case, for instance, of the woman who married three successive husbands, each of whom fell ill soon afterwards and had to be nursed by her on their death-beds.

The most moving poetic picture of a fate such as this is given by Tasso in his romantic epic *Gerusalemme Liberata*. Its hero, Tancred, unwittingly kills his beloved Clorinda in a duel while she is disguised in the armor of an enemy knight. After her burial, he makes his way into a strange magic forest which strikes the Crusaders' army with terror. He slashes with his sword at a tall tree; but blood streams from the cut and the voice of *Clorinda*, whose soul is imprisoned in the tree, is heard complaining that he has wounded his beloved once again.

If we take into account observations such as these, based upon behavior in the transference, and upon the life-histories of men and women, we shall find courage to assume that there really does exist, in the mind, a compulsion to repeat that overrides the pleasure principle. Now, too, we shall be inclined to relate to this compulsion the dreams that occur in traumatic neuroses and the impulse that leads children to play.

It is to be noted, however, that only in rare instances can we observe the pure effects of the compulsion to repeat, unsupported by other motives. In the case of children's play, we have already laid stress on the other ways in which the emergence of the compulsion may be interpreted; the compulsion to repeat and instinctual satisfaction that is immediately pleasurable, seem to converge here into an intimate partnership.

The phenomena of transference are obviously exploited by the resistance, which the ego maintains in its pertinacious insistence upon repression; the compulsion to repeat, which the treatment tries to bring into its service, is enticed over to its side, as it were, by the ego, clinging as it does to the pleasure principle.

A great deal of what might be described as the compulsion of destiny seems intelligible on a rational basis; so that we are under no necessity to call in a new and mysterious motive to explain it. The least dubious instance (of the presence of such a motive) is perhaps that of traumatic dreams. However, on mature reflection, we shall be forced to admit that even in the other instances, the whole ground is not covered by the operation of the familiar motives. Enough is left unexplained to justify the hypothesis of a compulsion to repeat something that seems more primitive, more elementary, more instinctual than the pleasure principle, which it sets aside.

But if a compulsion to repeat does operate in the mind, we should be glad to know something about it, to learn what function it corresponds to, under what conditions it can emerge, and what its relation is to the pleasure principle—to which, after all, we have hitherto ascribed dominance over the course of the processes of excitation in mental life.

Chapter Four

What follows is speculation, often far-fetched speculation, which the reader will consider or dismiss according to his individual predilection. It is further an attempt to follow out an idea consistently, out of curiosity to see where it will lead.

Psycho-analytic speculation takes, as its point of departure, the impression, derived from examining unconscious processes, that consciousness may be, not the most universal attribute of mental processes, but only a particular function of them. Speaking in meta-psychological terms, it asserts that consciousness is a function of a particular system which it describes as Cs.

What consciousness yields, consists essentially of perceptions of excitations coming from the external world, and of feelings of pleasure and unpleasure, which can only arise from within the mental apparatus. It is, therefore, possible to assign to the system Pcpt.-Cs. a position in space. It must lie on the borderline between outside and inside; it must be turned towards the external world and must envelop the other psychical systems.

It will be seen that there is nothing daringly new in these assumptions; we have merely adopted the views on localization held by cerebral anatomy, which locates the seat of consciousness in the cerebral cortex—the outermost, enveloping layer of the central organ.

Cerebral anatomy has no need to consider why, speaking anatomically, consciousness should be lodged on the surface of the brain, instead of being safely housed somewhere in its inmost interior. Perhaps *we* shall be more successful in accounting for this situation in the case of our system Pcpt.-Cs.

Consciousness is not the only distinctive character that we ascribe to the processes in that system. Based on impressions derived from our psychoanalytic experience, we assume that all excitatory processes that occur in the *other* systems leave permanent traces behind in them, which form the foundation of memory. Such memory traces, then, have nothing to do with the fact of becoming conscious; indeed they are often most powerful and most enduring when the process which left them behind was one that never entered consciousness.

We find it hard to believe, however, that permanent traces of excitation, such as these, are also left in the system Pcpt.-Cs. If they remained constantly conscious, they would very soon set limits to the system's aptitude for receiving fresh excitations.

If, on the other hand, they were unconscious, we should be faced with the problem of explaining the existence of unconscious processes in a system whose functioning was otherwise accompanied by the phenomenon of consciousness. We should, so to say, have altered nothing and gained nothing by our hypothesis relegating the process of becoming conscious to a special system. Though this consideration is not absolutely conclusive, it nevertheless leads us to suspect that becoming conscious and leaving behind a memory trace are processes incompatible with each other, within one and the same system.

Thus we should be able to say that the excitatory process becomes conscious in the system Cs. but leaves no permanent trace behind there; but that the excitation is transmitted to the systems lying next within, and that it is in *them* that its traces are left. I followed these same lines in the schematic picture, which I included in the speculative section of my *Interpretation of Dreams.*

It must be borne in mind that little enough is known from other sources of the origin of consciousness. When, therefore, we lay down the proposition that consciousness arises instead of a memory trace, the assertion deserves consideration, at all events on the ground of its being framed in fairly precise terms.

If this is so, the system Cs. is characterized by the peculiarity that in it (in contrast to what happens in the other psychical systems), excitatory processes do not leave behind any permanent change in its elements, but expire, as it were, in the phenomenon of becoming conscious.

An exception of this sort, to the general rule, requires to be explained by some factor that applies exclusively to that one system. Such a factor, which is absent in the other systems Cs. might well be the exposed situation of the system Cs., immediately abutting, as it does, on the external world.

Let us picture a living organism in its most simplified possible form as an undifferentiated vesicle of a substance that is susceptible to stimulation. Then, the surface turned toward the external world will, from its very situation, be differentiated and will serve as an organ for receiving stimuli. Indeed embryology, in its capacity as a recapitulation of developmental history, actually shows us that the central nervous system originates from the ectoderm. The grey matter of the cortex remains a derivative of the primitive superficial layer of the organism and may have inherited some of its essential properties.

It would be easy to suppose, then, that as a result of the ceaseless impact of external stimuli on the surface of the vesicle, its substance to a certain depth may have become permanently modified, so that excitatory processes run a different course in it from what they run in the deeper layers. A crust would thus be formed which would, at last, have been so thoroughly baked through, by stimulation, that it would present the most favorable possible conditions for the reception of stimuli, and become incapable of any further modification.

In terms of the system Cs., this would mean that its elements could undergo no further permanent modification from the passage of excitation, because they had already been modified in the respect in question to the greatest possible extent. Now, however, they would have become capable of giving rise to consciousness.

Various ideas may be formed that cannot, at present, be verified as to the nature of this modification of the substance and of the excitatory process. It may be supposed that, in passing from one element to another, an excitation has to overcome a resistance, and that the diminution of resistance thus effected is what lays down a permanent trace of the excitation, that is, a pathway.

In the system Cs., then, resistance, of this kind, to passage from one element to another, would no longer exist. This picture can be brought into relation with Breuer's distinction between quiescent (or bound) and mobile cathectic energy in the elements of the psychical systems. The elements of the system Cs. would carry no bound energy but only energy capable of free discharge. It seems best, however, to express oneself as cautiously as possible on these points. None the less, this speculation will have enabled us to bring the origin of consciousness into some sort of connection with the situation of the system Cs. and with the peculiarities that must be ascribed to the excitatory processes taking place in it.

But we have more to say of the living vesicle with its receptive cortical layer. This little fragment of living substance is suspended in the middle of an external world charged, with the most powerful energies. It would be killed by the stimulation emanating from these if it were not provided with a protective shield against stimuli.

It acquires the shield in this way: its outermost surface ceases to have the structure proper to living matter, becomes to some degree inorganic, and thenceforward functions as a special envelope or membrane resistant to stimuli. In consequence, the energies of the external world are able to pass into the next underlying layers, which have remained living, with only a fragment of their original intensity.

These layers can devote themselves, behind the protective shield, to the reception of the amounts of stimulus which have been allowed through it. By its death, the outer layer has saved all the deeper ones from a similar fate—unless, that is to say, stimuli reach it, which are so strong that they break through the protective shield.

Protection against stimuli is an almost more important function for the living organism than *reception* of stimuli. The protective shield is supplied with its own store of energy and must, above all, endeavor to preserve the special forms of conversion of energy operating in it, against the effects threatened by the enormous energies at work in the external world—effects which tend toward an equalization of potential and hence toward destruction.

The main purpose of the *reception* of stimuli is to discover the direction and nature of the external stimuli; and for that it is enough to take small specimens of the external world, to sample it in small quantities. In highly developed organisms, the receptive cortical layer of the former vesicle has long been withdrawn into the depths of the interior of the body, though portions of it have been left behind on the surface immediately beneath the general shield against stimuli.

These are the sense organs, which consist essentially of apparatus for the reception of certain specific effects of stimulation, but which also include special arrangements for further protection against excessive amounts of stimulation and for excluding unsuitable kinds of stimuli. It is characteristic of them that they deal only with very small quantities of external stimulation and only take in samples of the external world. They may, perhaps, be compared with feelers that are, all the time, making tentative advances towards the external world and then drawing back from it.

At this point, I shall venture to touch for a moment upon a subject which would merit the most exhaustive treatment. As a result of certain psycho-analytic discoveries, we are today in a position to embark on a discussion of the Kantian theorem that time and space are necessary forms of thought. We have learned that unconscious mental processes are in themselves timeless. This means, in the first place, that they are not ordered in time, that time does not change them in any way, and that the idea of time cannot be applied to them.

These are negative characteristics that can only be clearly understood if a comparison is made with *conscious* mental processes. On the other hand, our abstract idea of time seems to be wholly derived from the method of working of the system Pcpt.-Cs. and to correspond to a perception on its own part of that method of working. This mode of functioning may, perhaps, constitute another way of providing a shield against stimuli. I know that these remarks must sound very obscure, but I must limit myself to these hints.

We have pointed out how the living vesicle is provided with a shield against stimuli from the external world; and we had previously shown that the cortical layer next to that shield must be differentiated as an organ for receiving stimuli from without. This sensitive cortex, however, which is later to become the system Cs., also receives excitations from *within*. The situation of the system between the outside and the inside, and the difference between the conditions governing the reception of excitations in the two cases, have a decisive effect on the functioning of the system and of the whole mental apparatus.

Toward the outside, it is shielded against stimuli, and the amounts of excitation impinging on it have only a reduced effect. Toward the inside, there can be no such shield; the excitations in the deeper layers extend into the system directly and in undiminished amount, in so far as certain of their characteristics give rise to feelings in the pleasure-unpleasure series.

The excitations coming from within are, however, in their intensity and in other qualitative respects—in their amplitude, perhaps—more commensurate with the system's method of working than the stimuli that stream in from the external world.

This state of things produces two definite results. First, the feelings of pleasure and unpleasure (which are an index to what is happening in the interior of the apparatus) predominate over all external stimuli. And secondly, a particular way is adopted of dealing with any internal excitations that produce too great an increase of unpleasure: there is a tendency to treat them as though they were acting, not from the inside, but from the outside, so that it may be possible to bring the shield against stimuli into operation as a means of defense against them. This is the origin of *projection*, which is destined to play such a large part in the causation of pathological processes.

I have an impression that these last considerations have brought us to a better understanding of the dominance of the pleasure principle; but no light has yet been thrown on the cases that contradict that dominance. Let us therefore go a step further. We describe as traumatic, any excitations from outside powerful enough to break through the protective shield. It seems to me that the concept of trauma necessarily implies a connection of this kind with a breach in an otherwise efficacious barrier against stimuli.

Such an event as an external trauma is bound to provoke a disturbance on a large scale in the functioning of the organism's energy and to set in motion every possible defensive measure.

At the same time, the pleasure principle is for the moment put out of action. There is no longer any possibility of preventing the mental apparatus from being flooded with large amounts of stimulus, and another problem arises instead—the problem of mastering the amounts of stimulus that have broken in and of binding them, in the psychical sense, so that they can subsequently be discharged.

The specific unpleasure of physical pain is probably the result of the protective shield having been broken through in a limited area. There is, then, a continuous stream of excitations from the part of the periphery concerned to the central apparatus of the mind, such as could normally arise only from *within* the apparatus.

And how shall we expect the mind to react to this invasion? Cathectic energy is summoned from all sides to provide sufficiently high cathexes of energy in the environs of the breach. An anticathexis, on a grand scale, is set up for whose benefit all the other psychical systems are impoverished, so that the remaining psychical functions are extensively paralyzed or reduced.

We must endeavor to draw a lesson from examples such as this and use them as a basis for our metapsychological speculations. From the present case, then, we infer that a system, which is itself highly cathected, is capable of taking up an additional stream of fresh inflowing energy and of converting it into quiescent cathexis—that is of binding it psychically.

The higher the system's own quiescent cathexis, the greater seems to be its binding force. Conversely, therefore, the lower its cathexis, the less capacity it will have for taking up inflowing energy, and the more violent must be the consequences of such a breach in the protective shield against stimuli. To this view, it cannot be justly objected that the increase of cathexis, around the breach, can be explained far more simply as the direct result of the inflowing masses of excitation.

If that were so, the mental apparatus would merely receive an increase in its cathexes of energy, and the paralyzing character of pain and the impoverishment of all the other systems would remain unexplained. Nor do the very violent phenomena of discharge, to which pain gives rise, affect our explanation, for they occur in a reflex manner. That is, they follow without the intervention of the mental apparatus.

The indefiniteness of all our discussions on what we describe as meta-psychology is, of course, due to the fact that we know nothing of the nature of the excitatory process that takes place in the elements of the psychical systems, and that we do not feel justified in framing any hypothesis on the subject. We are, consequently, operating all the time with a large unknown quantity, which we are obliged to carry over into every new formula.

It may be reasonably supposed that this excitatory process can be carried out with energies that vary *quantitatively*; it may also seem probable that it has more than one *quality* (in the nature of amplitude, for instance). As a new factor, we have taken into consideration Breuer's hypothesis that charges of energy occur in two forms; so that we have to distinguish between two kinds of cathexis of the psychical systems or their elements—a freely flowing cathexis that presses on toward discharge, and a quiescent cathexis. We may suspect that the binding of the energy that streams into the mental apparatus consists, in its conversion, from a freely flowing into a quiescent state.

We may, I think, tentatively venture to regard the common traumatic neurosis as a consequence of an extensive breach being made in the protective shield against stimuli. This would seem to reinstate the old, naive theory of shock, in apparent contrast to the later and psychologically more pretentious theory, which attributes etiological importance not to the effects of mechanical violence, but to fright and the threat to life.

These opposing views are not, however, irreconcilable; nor is the psychoanalytic view of the traumatic neurosis identical with the shock theory in its crudest form. The latter regards the essence of the shock as being the direct damage to the molecular structure or even to the histological structure of the elements of the nervous system; whereas what *we* seek to understand are the effects produced on the organ of the mind by the breach in the shield against stimuli and by the problems that follow in its train.

But we too attribute importance to the element of fright. It is caused by the absence of any preparedness for anxiety, including a hypercathexis of the systems that would be the first to receive the stimulus. Owing to their low cathexis, those systems are not in a good position for binding the inflowing amounts of excitation, and the consequences of the breach in the protective shield follow all the more easily. It will be seen, then, that preparedness for anxiety and the hypercathexis of the receptive systems constitute the last line of defense of the shield against stimuli.

In the case of quite a number of traumas, the difference between systems that are unprepared and systems that are well prepared, through being hypercathected, may be a decisive factor in determining the outcome. Though where the strength of a trauma exceeds a certain limit, this factor will no doubt cease to carry weight.

The fulfillment of wishes is, as we know, brought about in a hallucinatory manner by dreams, and under the dominance of the pleasure principle, this has become their function. But it is not in the service of that principle that the dreams of patients suffering from traumatic neuroses lead them back with such regularity to the situation in which the trauma occurred. We may assume, rather, that dreams are, here, helping to carry out another task, which must be accomplished before the dominance of the pleasure principle can even begin.

These dreams are endeavoring to master the stimulus retrospectively, by developing the anxiety whose omission was the cause of the traumatic neurosis. They thus afford us a view of a function of the mental apparatus, which, though it does not contradict the pleasure principle, is nevertheless independent of it and seems to be more primitive than the purpose of gaining pleasure and avoiding unpleasure.

This would seem to be the place, then, at which to admit, for the first time, an exception to the proposition that dreams are fulfillments of wishes. Anxiety dreams, as I have shown repeatedly and in detail, offer no such exception. Nor do punishment dreams, for they merely replace the forbidden wish fulfillment with the appropriate punishment for it. That is to say, they fulfill the wish of the sense of guilt, which is the reaction to the repudiated impulse.

But it is impossible to classify as wish-fulfillments the dreams we have been discussing that occur in traumatic neuroses, or the dreams during psychoanalyses, which bring to memory the psychical traumas of childhood. They arise, rather, in obedience to the compulsion to repeat, though it is true that, in analysis, that compulsion is supported by the wish (which is encouraged by suggestion) to conjure up what has been forgotten and repressed.

Thus, it would seem that the function of dreams, which consists in setting aside any motives that might interrupt sleep, by fulfilling the wishes of the disturbing impulses, is not their *original* function. It would not be possible for them to perform that function until the whole of mental life had accepted the dominance of the pleasure principle.

If there is a *beyond the pleasure principle,* it is only consistent to grant that there was also a time before the purpose of dreams was the fulfillment of wishes. This would imply no denial of their later function. But, if once, this general rule has been broken, a further question arises. May not dreams which, with a view to the psychical binding of traumatic impressions, obey the compulsion to repeat—may not such dreams occur *outside* analysis as well? And the reply can only be a decided affirmative.

I have argued, elsewhere, that the war neuroses (in so far as that term implies something more than a reference to the circumstances of the illness's onset) may very well be traumatic neuroses thathave been facilitated by a conflict in the ego.

The fact to which I have referred, that a gross physical injury caused simultaneously by the trauma, diminishes the chances that a neurosis will develop, becomes intelligible if one bears in mind two facts, which have been stressed by psychoanalytic research. Firstly, that mechanical agitation must be recognized as one of the sources of sexual excitation, and secondly, that painful and feverish illnesses exercise a powerful effect, so long as they last, on the distribution of libido.

Thus, on the one hand, the mechanical violence of the trauma would liberate a quantity of sexual excitation which, owing to the lack of preparation for anxiety, would have a traumatic effect. On the other hand, the simultaneous physical injury, by calling for a narcissistic hypercathexis of the injured organ, would bind the excess of excitation.

It is also well known, though the libido theory has not yet made sufficient use of the fact, that such severe disorders in the distribution of libido as melancholia are temporarily brought to an end by intercurrent organic illness, and indeed that even a fully developed condition of dementia praecox is capable of a temporary remission in these same circumstances.

Chapter Five

The fact that the cortical layer, which receives stimuli, is without any protective shield against excitations from within must have, as its result, that these latter transmissions of stimulus have a preponderance in economic importance and often occasion economic disturbances comparable with traumatic neuroses. The most abundant sources of this internal excitation are what are described as the organism's instincts—the representatives of all the forces originating in the interior of the body and transmitted to the mental apparatus—at once the most important and the most obscure element of psychological research.

It will, perhaps, not be thought too rash to suppose that the impulses arising from the instincts do not belong to the type of *bound* nervous processes but to the type of *mobile* processes that press towards discharge. The best part of what we know of these processes is derived from our study of the dream activity. We there discovered that the processes in the unconscious systems were fundamentally different from those in the preconscious (or conscious) systems. In the unconscious, cathexes can easily be completely transferred, displaced, and condensed.

Such treatment, however, could only produce invalid results if it were applied to preconscious material. This accounts for the familiar peculiarities exhibited by manifest dreams after the preconscious residues of the preceding day have been worked over in accordance with the laws operating in the unconscious. I described the type of process found in the unconscious as the primary psychical process, in contra-distinction to the secondary process, which is the one obtaining in our normal waking life.

Because all instinctual impulses have the unconscious systems as their point of impact, it is hardly an innovation to say that they obey the primary process. Again, it is not difficult to identify the primary psychical process with Breuer's mobile cathexis and the secondary process with changes in his bound or tonic cathexis. If so, it would be the task of the higher strata of the mental apparatus to bind the instinctual excitation reaching the primary process.

A failure to effect this binding would provoke a disturbance analogous to a traumatic neurosis; and only after the binding has been accomplished would it be possible for the dominance of the pleasure principle (and of its modification, the reality principle) to proceed unhindered. Until then, the other task of the mental apparatus, the task of mastering or binding excitations, would have precedence—not, indeed, in *opposition* to the pleasure principle, but independently of it and to some extent in disregard of it.

The manifestations of a compulsion to repeat (which we have described as occurring in the early activities of infantile mental life, as well as among the events of psycho-analytic treatment) exhibit, to a high degree, an instinctual character. When they act in opposition to the pleasure principle, they give the appearance of some extraneous force at work.

In the case of children's play, we seemed to see that children repeat unpleasurable experiences for the additional reason that they can master a powerful impression, far more thoroughly, by being active than they could by merely experiencing it passively. Each fresh repetition seems to strengthen the mastery they are in search of.

Nor can children have their pleasurable experiences repeated often enough, and they are inexorable in their insistence that the repetition shall be an identical one. This character trait disappears later on. If a joke is heard for a second time, it produces almost no effect; a theatrical production never creates so great an impression the second time as the first. Indeed, it is hardly possible to persuade an adult who has very much enjoyed reading a book to re-read it immediately.

Novelty is always the condition of enjoyment. But children will never tire of asking an adult to repeat a game that he has shown them or played with them, until he is too exhausted to go on. And if a child has been told a nice story, he will insist on hearing it over and over again, rather than a new one. He will remorselessly stipulate that the repetition shall be an identical one, and will correct any alterations of which the narrator may be guilty—though they may actually have been made in the hope of gaining fresh approval.

None of this contradicts the pleasure principle. Repetition, the re-experiencing of something identical, is clearly in itself a source of pleasure. In the case of a person in analysis, on the contrary, the compulsion to repeat the events of his childhood in the transference evidently disregards the pleasure principle in every way. The patient behaves in a purely infantile fashion and, thus, shows us that the repressed memory-traces of his primeval experiences are not present in him in a bound state, and are indeed, in a sense, incapable of obeying the secondary process.

It is to this fact of not being bound, moreover, that they owe their capacity for forming, in conjunction with the residues of the previous day, a wishful fantasy that emerges in a dream. This same compulsion to repeat frequently meets us as an obstacle to our treatment, when, at the end of an analysis, we try to induce the patient to detach himself completely from his physician. It may be presumed, too, that when people unfamiliar with analysis feel an obscure fear—a dread of rousing something that, so they feel, is better left sleeping—what they are afraid of, at bottom, is the emergence of this compulsion with its hint of possession by some extraneous power.

But how is the predicate of being instinctual related to the compulsion to repeat? At this point, we cannot escape a suspicion that we may have come upon the track of a universal attribute of the instincts and perhaps of organic life, in general, which has not hitherto been clearly recognized or, at least, not explicitly stressed. It seems, then, that an instinct is a compulsion inherent in organic life to restore an earlier state of things, which the living entity has been obliged to abandon under the pressure of external disturbing forces. That is, it is a kind of organic elasticity, or, to put it another way, the expression of the inertia inherent in organic life.

This view of instincts strikes us as strange because we have become used to see, in them, a factor impelling toward change and development, whereas we are now asked to recognize, in them, the precise contrary—an expression of the *conservative* nature of living substance. On the other hand, we soon call to mind examples from animal life that seem to confirm the view that instincts are historically determined.

Certain fish, for instance, undertake laborious migrations at spawning-time, in order to deposit their spawn in particular waters far removed from their customary haunts. In the opinion of many biologists, what they are doing is merely to seek out the localities in which their species formerly resided but which, in the course of time, they have exchanged for others.

The same explanation is believed to apply to the migratory flights of birds of passage. We are quickly relieved of the necessity for seeking for further examples by the reflection that the most impressive proofs of there being an organic compulsion to repeat, lie in the phenomena of heredity and the facts of embryology.

We see how the germ of a living animal is obliged, in the course of its development, to recapitulate (even if only in a transient and abbreviated fashion) the structures of all the forms from which it is sprung, instead of proceeding quickly by the shortest path to its final shape. This behavior is only to a very slight degree attributable to mechanical causes. The historical explanation cannot accordingly be neglected. So, too, the power of regenerating a lost organ by growing afresh a precisely similar one, extends far up into the animal kingdom.

We shall be met by the plausible objection that it may very well be that, in addition to the conservative instincts that impel toward repetition, there may be others that push forward toward progress and the production of new forms. This argument must certainly not be overlooked, and it will be taken into account at a later stage. But for the moment, it is tempting to pursue the hypothesis that all instincts tend toward the restoration of an earlier state of things to its logical conclusion.

The outcome may give an impression of mysticism or of sham profundity; but we can feel quite innocent of having had any such purpose in view. We seek only for the sober results of research or of reflection based on it; and we have no wish to find, in those results, any quality other than certainty.

Let us suppose, then, that all the organic instincts are conservative, are acquired historically, and tend toward the restoration of an earlier state of things. It follows that the phenomena of organic development must be attributed to external disturbing and diverting influences. The elementary living entity would, from its very beginning, have had no wish to change; if conditions remained the same, it would do no more than constantly repeat the same course of life. (The reader should not overlook the fact that what follows is the development of an extreme line of thought. Later on, when account is taken of the sexual instincts, it will be found that the necessary limitations and corrections are applied to it.)

In the last resort, what has left its mark on the development of organisms, must be the history of the earth we live in and of its relation to the sun. Every modification, that is thus imposed upon the course of the organism's life, is accepted by the conservative organic instincts and stored up for further repetition. Those instincts are, therefore, bound to give a deceptive appearance of being forces tending toward change and progress, while, in fact, they are merely seeking to reach an ancient goal by paths alike old and new.

Moreover, it is possible to specify this final goal of all organic striving. It would be in contradiction to the conservative nature of the instincts if the goal of life were a state of things that had never yet been attained. On the contrary, it must be an *old* state of things, an initial state from which the living entity has, at one time or other, departed, and to which it is striving to return by the circuitous paths along which its development leads.

If we are to take it as a truth that knows no exception that everything living dies for *internal* reasons—becomes inorganic once again—then we shall be compelled to say that "the goal of all life is death" and, looking backward, that what was inanimate existed before what is living.

The attributes of life were, at some time, evoked in inanimate matter by the action of a force of whose nature we can form no conception. It may, perhaps, have been a process similar in type to that which later caused the development of consciousness in a particular stratum of living matter. The tension, which then arose in what had previously been an inanimate substance, endeavored to equalize its potential.

In this way, the first instinct came into being: the instinct to return to the inanimate state. It was still an easy matter, at that time, for a living substance to die. The course of its life was probably only a brief one, whose direction was determined by the chemical structure of the young life. For a long time, perhaps, living substance was thus being constantly created afresh and easily dying, until decisive external influences altered in such a way as to oblige the still surviving substance to diverge ever more widely from its original course of life and to make ever more complicated detours before reaching its goal in death.

These circuitous paths to death, faithfully kept to by the conservative instincts, would present us today with the picture of the phenomena of life. If we firmly maintain the exclusively conservative nature of instincts, we cannot arrive at any other notions as to the origin and goal of life.

The implications, concerning the great groups of instincts, which, as we believe, lie behind the phenomena of life in organisms, must appear no less bewildering. The hypothesis of self-preservative instincts, such as we attribute to all living beings, stands in marked opposition to the idea that instinctual life, as a whole, serves to bring about death.

Seen in this light, the theoretical importance of the instincts of self-preservation, of self-assertion, and of mastery greatly diminishes. They are component instincts whose function it is to assure that the organism shall follow its own path to death, and to ward off any possible ways of returning to inorganic existence, other than those that are immanent in the organism itself.

We have no longer to reckon with the organism's puzzling determination (so hard to fit into any context) to maintain its own existence in the face of every obstacle. What we are left with is the fact that the organism wishes to die only in its own fashion. Thus, these guardians of life, too, were originally the myrmidons of death. Hence arises the paradoxical situation that the living organism struggles most energetically against events (dangers, in fact) that might help it to attain its life's goal rapidly—by a kind of short-circuit. Such behavior is, however, precisely what characterizes instinctual as contrasted with intelligent efforts.

But let us pause for a moment and reflect. It cannot be so. The sexual instincts, to which the theory of the neuroses gives a quite special place, appear under a very different aspect.

The external pressure, which provokes a constantly increasing extent of development, has not imposed itself upon *every* organism. Many have succeeded in remaining, up to the present time, at their lowly level. Many, if not all, of such creatures, which are living today, must resemble the earliest stages of the higher animals and plants.

In the same way, the whole path of development to natural death is not trodden by *all* the elementary entities that compose the complicated body of one of the higher organisms. Some of them, the germ-cells, probably retain the original structure of living matter and, after a certain time, with their full complement of inherited and freshly acquired instinctual dispositions, separate themselves from the organism as a whole.

These two characteristics may be precisely what enable them to have an independent existence. Under favorable conditions, they begin to develop—that is, to repeat the performance to which they owe their existence. In the end, once again, one portion of their substance pursues its development to a finish, while another portion harks back, once again, as a fresh residual germ to the beginning of the process of development.

These germ-cells, therefore, work against the death of the living substance and succeed in winning, for it, what we can only regard as potential immortality, though that may mean no more than a lengthening of the road to death. We must regard, as in the highest degree significant, the fact that this function of the germ-cell is reinforced, or only made possible, if it coalesces with another cell similar to itself and yet differing from it.

The instincts that watch over the destinies of these elementary organisms that survive the whole individual, which provide them with a safe shelter while they are defenseless against the stimuli of the external world, which bring about their meeting with other germ-cells, and so on—these constitute the group of the sexual instincts. They are conservative in the same sense as the other instincts in that they bring back earlier states of living substance; but they are conservative to a higher degree, in that they are peculiarly resistant to external influences.

They are conservative, too, in another sense, in that they preserve life itself for a comparatively long period. Yet it is to them, alone, that we can attribute an internal impulse toward progress and toward higher development! They are the true life instincts. They operate against the purpose of the other instincts, which leads, by reason, of their function to death; and this fact indicates that there is an opposition between them and the other instincts, an opposition whose importance was long ago recognized by the theory of the neuroses.

It is as though the life of the organism moved with a vacillating rhythm. One group of instincts rushes forward, to reach the final goal of life as swiftly as possible; but when a particular stage in the advance has been reached, the other group jerks back to a certain point to make a fresh start and so prolong the journey. Even though it is certain that sexuality and the distinction between the sexes did not exist when life began, the possibility remains that the instincts, which were later to be described as sexual, may have been in operation from the very start. It may not be true that it was only at a later time that they started upon their work of opposing the activities of the ego instincts.

Let us now hark back, for a moment, ourselves, and consider whether there is any basis at all for these speculations. Is it really the case that, apart from the sexual instincts, there are no instincts that do not seek to restore an earlier state of things? That there are none that aim at a state of things which has never yet been attained?

I know of no certain example, from the organic world, that would contradict the characterization I have thus proposed. There is, unquestionably, no universal instinct toward higher development observable in the animal or plant world, even though it is undeniable that development does, in fact, occur in that direction. But, on the one hand, it is often merely a matter of opinion when we declare that, one stage of development, is higher than another; and on the other hand, biology teaches us that higher development, in one respect, is very frequently balanced or outweighed by involution in another.

Moreover, there are plenty of animal forms, from whose early stages we can infer, that their development has, on the contrary, assumed a retrograde character. Both higher development and involution might well be the consequences of adaptation to the pressure of external forces; and in both cases the part played by instincts might be limited to the retention (in the form of an internal source of pleasure) of an obligatory modification.

It may be difficult, too, for many of us, to abandon the belief that there is an instinct toward perfection at work in human beings, which has brought them to their present high level of intellectual achievement and ethical sublimation, and which may be expected to watch over their development into supermen.

I have no faith, however, in the existence of any such internal instinct, and I cannot see how this benevolent illusion is to be preserved. The present development of human beings requires, as it seems to me, no different explanation from that of animals. What appears in a minority of human individuals as an untiring impulsion toward further perfection, can easily be understood as a result of the instinctual repression upon, which is based, all that is most precious in human civilization.

The repressed instinct never ceases to strive for complete satisfaction, which would consist in the repetition of a primary experience of satisfaction. No substitutive or reactive formations and no sublimations will suffice to remove the repressed instinct's persisting tension. It is the difference in amount between the gratificatory pleasure, which is demanded, and that which is actually achieved, that provides the driving factor that will permit of no halting, at any established position.

The backward path that leads to complete satisfaction is, as a rule, obstructed by the resistances that maintain the repressions. So there is no alternative but to advance in the direction in which growth is still free—though with no prospect of bringing the process to a conclusion or of being able to reach the goal.

The processes involved in the formation of a neurotic phobia, which is nothing else than an attempt at flight from the satisfaction of an instinct, present us with a model of the manner of origin of this supposititious instinct towards perfection—an instinct which cannot possibly be attributed to *every* human being. The *dynamic* conditions for its development are, indeed, universally present; but it is only in rare cases that the *economic* situation appears to favor the production of the phenomenon.

I will add only a word to suggest that the efforts of Eros, to combine organic substances into ever larger unities, probably provide a substitute for this instinct towards perfection, whose existence we cannot admit. The phenomena that are attributed to it seem capable of explanation by these efforts of Eros, taken in conjunction with the results of repression.

Chapter Six

The upshot of our enquiry, so far, has been the drawing of a sharp distinction between the ego instincts and the sexual instincts, and the view that the former exercise a thrust toward death, and the latter towards a prolongation of life. But this conclusion is bound to be unsatisfactory in many respects, even to ourselves. Moreover, it is actually only of the former group of instincts, that we can predicate a conservative, or rather retrograde, character corresponding to a compulsion to repeat.

For on our hypothesis the ego instincts arise from the coming to life of inanimate matter, and they seek to restore the inanimate state. Whereas as regards the sexual instincts, though it is true that they reproduce primitive states of the organism, what they are clearly aiming at, by every possible means, is the coalescence of two germ-cells that are differentiated in a particular way.

If this union is not effected, the germ-cell dies along with all the other elements of the multi-cellular organism. It is only on this condition that the sexual function can prolong the cell's life and lend it the appearance of immortality. But what is the important event in the development of living substance that is being repeated in sexual reproduction, or in its fore-runner, the conjugation of two protista?

We cannot say, and we should, consequently, feel relieved if the whole structure of our argument turned out to be mistaken. The opposition between the ego or death instincts and the sexual, or life instincts, would then cease to hold, and the compulsion to repeat would no longer possess the importance we have ascribed to it.

Let us turn back, then, to one of the assumptions that we have already made, with the expectation that we shall be able to give it a categorical denial. We have drawn far-reaching conclusions from the hypothesis that all living substance is bound to die from internal causes.

We made this assumption thus carelessly, because it does not seem to us to *be* an assumption.

We are accustomed to think that such is the fact, and we are strengthened in our thought by the writings of our poets. Perhaps we have adopted the belief because there is some comfort in it. If we are to die ourselves, and first to lose in death those who are dearest to us, it is easier to submit to a remorseless law of nature, to the sublime than to a chance that might have been escaped.

It may be, however, that this belief in the internal necessity of dying is only another of those illusions we have created, *to bear the burden of existence*. It is certainly not a primeval belief. The notion of natural death is quite foreign to primitive races; they attribute every death that occurs, among them, to the influence of an enemy or of an evil spirit.

We must, therefore, turn to biology in order to test the validity of the belief. If we do so, we may be astonished to find how little agreement there is among biologists on the subject of natural death and, in fact, that the whole concept of death melts away under their hands. The fact that there is a fixed average duration of life, at least among the higher animals, naturally argues in favor of there being such a thing as death from natural causes.

But this impression is countered when we consider that certain large animals and certain gigantic arboreal growths reach a very advanced age, and one that cannot, at present, be computed. According to the grandiose conception of Wilhelm Fliess (1906), all the vital phenomena exhibited by organisms—including, no doubt, their death—are linked with the completion of fixed periods, which express the dependence of two kinds of living substance (one male and the other female) upon the solar year.

When we see, however, how easily and how extensively the influence of external forces is able to modify the date of the appearance of vital phenomena (especially in the plant world), to precipitate them or hold them back—doubts must be cast upon the rigidity of Fliess's formulas, or at least, upon whether the laws laid down by him are the sole determining factors.

The greatest interest attaches from our point of view to the treatment given to the subject of the duration of life and the death of organisms in the writings of Weismann (1882, 1884, 1892, etc.) It was he who introduced the division of living substance into mortal and immortal parts.

The mortal part is the body in the narrower sense—the soma, which alone is subject to natural death. The germ cells, on the other hand, are potentially immortal, in so far as they are able, under certain favorable conditions, to develop into a new individual, or, in other words, to surround themselves with a new soma (Weismann, 1884).

What strikes us, in this, is the unexpected analogy with our own view, which was arrived at along such a different path. Weismann, regarding living substance morphologically, sees in it one portion that is destined to die—the soma, the body apart from the substance concerned with sex and inheritance and an immortal portion—the germ-plasm, which is concerned with the survival of the species, with reproduction.

We, on the other hand, dealing not with the living substance, but with the forces operating in it, have been led to distinguish two kinds of instincts: those which seek to lead what is living to death, and others, the sexual instincts, which are perpetually attempting and achieving a renewal of life. This sounds like a dynamic corollary to Weismann's morphological theory.

But the appearance of a significant correspondence is dissipated as soon as we discover

Weismann's views on the problem of death. For he only relates the distinction between the mortal soma and the immortal germ-plasm to *multicellular* organisms. In unicellular organisms the individual and the reproductive cell are still one and the same (Weismann, 1882).

Thus, he considers that unicellular organisms are potentially immortal, and that death only makes its appearance with the multicellular metazoa. It is true that this death of the higher organisms is a natural one, a death from internal causes; but it is not founded upon any primal characteristic of living substance (Weismann, 1884), and cannot be regarded as an absolute necessity with its basis in the very nature of life (Weismann, 1882).

Death is, rather, a matter of expediency, a manifestation of adaptation to the external conditions of life. For, when once the cells of the body have been divided into soma and germ-plasm, an unlimited duration of individual life would become a quite pointless luxury. When this differentiation had been made in the multicellular organisms, death became possible and expedient.

Because, then, the soma of the higher organisms has died at fixed periods for internal reasons, while the protista have remained immortal. It is not the case, on the other hand, that reproduction was only introduced at the same time as death. On the contrary, it is a primal characteristic of living matter, like growth (from which it originated), and life has been continuous from its first beginning upon earth (Weismann, 1884).

It will be seen, at once, that to concede in this way that higher organisms have a natural death, is of very little help to us. If death is a late acquisition of organisms, then there can be no question of there having been death instincts from the very beginning of life on this earth.

Multi-cellular organisms may die for internal reasons, owing to defective differentiation or to imperfections in their metabolism, but the matter is of no interest from the point of view of our problem. An account of the origin of death, such as this, is, moreover, far less at variance with our habitual modes of thought than the strange assumption of death instincts.

The discussion, which followed upon Weismann's suggestions, led, so far as I can see, to no conclusive results in any direction. Some writers returned to the views of Goette (1883), who regarded death as a direct result of reproduction.

Hartmann (1906) does not regard the appearance of a dead body a dead portion of the living substance—as the criterion of death, but defines death as "the termination of individual development."

In this sense, protozoa too are mortal. In their case, death always coincides with reproduction, but is to some extent obscured by it, since the whole substance of the parent animal may be transmitted directly into the young offspring.

Soon afterward, research was directed to the experimental testing upon unicellular organisms of the alleged immortality of living substance. An American biologist, Woodruff, experimenting with a ciliate infusorian, the "slipper-animalcule," which reproduces by fission into two individuals, persisted until the 3029th generation (at which point he broke off the experiment), isolating one of the part products on each occasion and placing it in fresh water.

This remote descendent of the first slipper-animalcule was just as lively as its ancestor was, and showed no signs of ageing or degeneration. Thus, in so far as figures of this kind prove anything, the immortality of the protista seemed to be experimentally demonstrable.

Other experimenters arrived at different results. Maupas, Calkins, and others, in contrast to Woodruff, found that after a certain number of divisions, these infusoria become weaker, diminish in size, suffer the loss of some part of their organization, and eventually die—unless certain recuperative measures are applied to them.

If this is so, protozoa would appear to die after a phase of senescence exactly like the higher animals—thus completely contradicting the assertion that death is a late acquisition of living organisms.

From the aggregate of these experiments, two facts emerge that seem to offer us a firm footing. First: If two of the animalculae, at the moment before they show signs of senescence, are able to coalesce with each other, that is to conjugate, (soon after which they once more separate), they are saved from growing old and become rejuvenated.

Conjugation is no doubt the fore-runner of the sexual reproduction of higher creatures; it is as yet unconnected with propagation and is limited to the mixing of the substances of the two individuals. The recuperative effects of conjugation can, however, be replaced by certain stimulating agents, by alterations in the composition of the fluid that provides their nourishment, by raising their temperature or by shaking them.

We are reminded of the celebrated experiment made by J. Loeb, in which, by means of certain chemical stimuli, he induced segmentation in sea-urchins' eggs—a process which can normally occur only after fertilization.

Second: It is probable, nevertheless, that infusoria die a natural death as a result of their own vital processes. For the contradiction between Woodruff's findings, and the others, is due to his having provided each generation with fresh nutrient fluid.

If he omitted to do so, he observed the same signs of senescence as the other experimenters. He concluded that the animalculae were injured by the products of metabolism, which they extruded into the surrounding fluid. He was then able to prove, conclusively, that it was only the products of its *own* metabolism that had fatal results for a particular generation.

For the same animalculae, which inevitably perished if they were crowded together in their own nutrient fluid, flourished in a solution that was over-saturated with the waste products of a distantly related species. An infusorian, therefore, if it is left to itself, dies a natural death owing to its incomplete voidance of the products of its own metabolism. It may be, however, that the same incapacity is the ultimate cause of the death of all higher animals as well.

At this point, the question may well arise in our minds whether any object, what-so-ever, is served by trying to solve the problem of natural death from a study of the protozoa. The primitive organization of these creatures may conceal, from our eyes, important conditions which, though in fact present in them too, only become *visible* in higher animals where they are able to find morphological expression. If we abandon the morphological point of view and adopt the dynamic one, it becomes a matter of complete indifference to us whether natural death can be shown to occur in protozoa or not.

The substance, which is later recognized as being immortal, has not yet become separated in them from the mortal one. The instinctual forces, which seek to conduct life into death, may also be operating in protozoa from the first, and yet their effects may be so completely concealed by the life-preserving forces, that it may be very hard to find any direct evidence of their presence.

We have seen, moreover, that the observations made by biologists allow us to assume that internal processes, of this kind, leading to death, do occur also in protista. But, even if protista turned out to be immortal in Weismann's sense, his assertion that death is a late acquisition would apply only to its *manifest* phenomena and would not make impossible the assumption of processes *tending* toward it.

Thus, our expectation that biology would flatly contradict the recognition of death instincts has not been fulfilled. We are at liberty to continue concerning ourselves with their possibility, if we have other reasons for doing so. The striking similarity between Weismann's distinction of soma and germ-plasm, and our separation of the death instincts from the life instincts, persists and retains its significance.

Let us pause, for a moment, over this pre-eminently dualistic view of instinctual life. According to E. Hering's theory, two kinds of processes are constantly at work in living substance, operating in contrary directions, one constructive or assimilatory, and the other destructive or dissimilatory.

May we venture to recognize, in these two directions taken by the vital processes, the activity of our two instinctual impulses, the life instincts and the death instincts? There is something else, at any rate, that we cannot remain blind to. We have unwittingly steered our course into the harbor of Schopenhauer's philosophy. For him, death is the "true result and to that extent the purpose of life," while the sexual instinct is the embodiment of the will to live.

Let us make a bold attempt at another step forward. It is generally considered that the union of a number of cells into a vital association—the multi-cellular character of organisms—has become a means of prolonging their life. One cell helps to preserve the life of another, and the community of cells can survive, even if individual cells have to die.

We have already heard that conjugation, too, the temporary coalescence of two unicellular organisms, has a life-preserving and rejuvenating effect on both of them. Accordingly, we might attempt to apply the libido theory, which has been arrived at in psychoanalysis, to the mutual relationship of cells.

We might suppose that the life instincts, or sexual instincts that are active in each cell, take the other cells as their object, that they partly neutralize the death instincts (the processes set up by them) in those other cells and, thus, preserve their life; while the other cells do the same for *them*, and still others sacrifice themselves in the performance of this libidinal function.

The germ-cells, themselves, would behave in a completely narcissistic fashion—to use the phrase that we are accustomed to use in the theory of the neuroses to describe a whole individual who retains his libido in his ego and pays none of it out in object-cathexes.

The germ-cells require their libido, the activity of their life instincts, for themselves, as a reserve against their later momentous constructive activity. The cells of the malignant neoplasms, which destroy the organism, should also be described as narcissistic in this same sense: pathology is prepared to regard their germs as innate and to ascribe embryonic attributes to them. In this way, the libido of our sexual instincts would coincide with the Eros of the poets and philosophers that binds all living things together.

Here, then, is an opportunity for looking back over the slow development of our libido theory. In the first instance, the analysis of the transference neuroses, forced upon our notice, the opposition between the sexual instincts, which are directed toward an object, and certain other instincts, with which we were very insufficiently acquainted, and which we described, provisionally, as the ego instincts.

A foremost place among these was necessarily given to the instincts serving the self-preservation of the individual. It was impossible to say what other distinctions were to be drawn among them. No knowledge would have been more valuable, as a foundation for true psychological knowledge, than an approximate grasp of the common characteristics and possible distinctive features of the instincts. But in no region of psychology were we groping more in the dark.

Everyone assumed the existence of as many instincts or, basic instincts, as he chose, and juggled with them like the ancient Greek natural philosophers with their four elements—earth, air, fire, and water. Psychoanalysis, which could not escape making *some* assumption about the instincts, kept, at first, to the popular division of instincts typified in the phrase "hunger and love." At least, there was nothing arbitrary in this; and by its help, the analysis of the psycho-neuroses was carried forward quite a distance.

The concept of sexuality, and, at the same time, of the sexual instinct, had, it is true, to be extended to cover many things that could not be classed under the reproductive function; and this caused no little hubbub in an austere, respectable, or merely hypocritical world.

The next step was taken when psychoanalysis felt its way closer toward the ego of psychology, which it had first come to know only as a repressive, censoring agency, capable of erecting protective structures and reactive formations.

Critical and far-seeing minds had, it is true, long since objected to the concept of libido being restricted to the energy of the sexual instincts directed towards an object. But they failed to explain how they had arrived at their better knowledge, or, to derive from it, anything of which analysis could make use.

Advancing more cautiously, psychoanalysis observed the regularity with which libido is withdrawn from the object and directed on to the ego (the process of introversion); and, by studying the libidinal development of children in its earliest phases, came to the conclusion that the ego is the true and original reservoir of libido, and that it is only from that reservoir that libido is extended on to objects.

The ego found its way among the child's sexual objects and was, at once given, the foremost place among them. Libido, which was in this way lodged in the ego, was described as narcissistic.

This narcissistic libido was, of course, also a manifestation of the force of the sexual instinct in the analytical sense of those words, and it had, necessarily, to be identified with the self-preservative instincts, whose existence had been recognized from the first.

Thus, the original opposition between the ego instincts and the sexual instincts proved to be inadequate. A portion of the ego instincts was seen to be libidinal; sexual instincts—probably alongside others—operated in the ego. Nevertheless, we are justified in saying that the old formula, which lays it down that psycho-neuroses are based on a conflict between ego instincts and sexual instincts, contains nothing that we need reject today. It is merely that the distinction between the two kinds of instinct, which was originally regarded as in some sort of way *qualitative*, must now be characterized differently, namely as being *topographical*. And in particular, it is still true that the transference neuroses, the essential subject of psycho-analytic study, are the result of a conflict between the ego and the libidinal cathexis of objects.

But it is all the more necessary for us to lay stress upon the libidinal character of the self-preservative instincts, now that we are venturing upon the further step of recognizing the sexual instinct as Eros, the preserver of all things, and of deriving the narcissistic libido of the ego, from the stores of libido—by means, of which, the cells of the soma are attached to one another.

But we now find ourselves suddenly faced by another question. If the self-preservative instincts, too, are of a libidinal nature, are there perhaps no other instincts whatever but the libidinal ones? At all events, there are none other visible. But, in that case, we shall, after all, be driven to agree with the critics who suspected, from the first, that psychoanalysis explains *everything* by sexuality, or with innovators like Jung, who, making a hasty judgment, have used the word libido to mean instinctual force in general. Must not this be so?

It was not our *intention,* at all events, to produce such a result. Our argument had, as its point of departure, a sharp distinction between ego instincts (which we equated with death instincts), and sexual instincts (which we equated with life instincts). We were prepared, at one stage, to include the, so-called, self-preservative instincts of the ego among the death instincts; but we subsequently corrected ourselves on this point and withdrew it.

Our views have, from the very first, been *dualistic*, and today they are even more definitely dualistic than before—now that we describe the opposition as being, not between ego instincts and sexual instincts, but between life instincts and death instincts.

Jung's libido theory is, on the contrary, *monistic*; the fact that he has called his one instinctual force "libido," is bound to cause confusion, but need not affect us otherwise. We suspect that instincts, other than those of self-preservation, operate in the ego, and it ought to be possible for us to point to them. Unfortunately, however, the analysis of the ego has made so little headway that it is very difficult for us to do so. It is possible, indeed, that the libidinal instincts in the ego may be linked in a peculiar manner with the other ego instincts that are still strange to us.

Even before we had any clear understanding of narcissism, psycho-analysts had a suspicion that the ego instincts had libidinal components attached to them. But these are very uncertain possibilities, to which our opponents will pay very little attention. The difficulty remains that psychoanalysis has not enabled us, until now, to point to any instincts other than the libidinal ones. That, however, is no reason for our falling in with the conclusion that no others, in fact, exist.

In the obscurity that reigns, at present, in the theory of the instincts, it would be unwise to reject any idea that promises to throw light on it. We started out, from the great opposition, between the life and death instincts. Now, object-love itself presents us with a second example of a similar polarity—that between love (or affection) and hate (or aggressiveness).

If only we could succeed in relating these two polarities to each other and in deriving one from the other! From the very first, we recognized the presence of a sadistic component in the sexual instinct. As we know, it can make itself independent and can, in the form of a perversion, dominate an individual's entire sexual activity.

It also emerges as a predominant component instinct in one of the pre-genital organizations, as I have named them. But how can the sadistic instinct, whose aim it is to injure the object, be derived from Eros, the preserver of life? Is it not plausible to suppose that this sadism is, in fact, a death instinct which, under the influence of the narcissistic libido, has been forced out of the ego and has consequently emerged in relation to the object? It now enters the service of the sexual function.

During the oral stage of organization of the libido, the act of obtaining erotic possession of an object coincides with that object's destruction; later, the sadistic instinct separates off, and finally, at the stage of genital primacy, it takes on, for the purposes of reproduction, the function of overpowering the sexual object to the extent necessary for carrying out the sexual act.

It might, indeed, be said that the sadism, which has been forced out of the ego, has pointed the way for the libidinal components of the sexual instinct, and that these follow after it to the object. Wherever the original sadism has undergone no mitigation or intermixture, we find the familiar ambivalence of love and hate in erotic life.

If such an assumption as this is permissible, then we have met the demand that we should produce an example of a death instinct—though it is true that our example is a displaced one. But, this way of looking at things is very far from being easy to grasp and creates a positively mystical impression. It looks, suspiciously, as though we were trying to find a way out of a highly embarrassing situation at any price.

We may recall, however, that there is nothing new in an assumption of this kind. We put one forward on an earlier occasion, before there was any question of an embarrassing situation. Clinical observations led us, at that time, to the view that masochism, the component instinct that is complementary to sadism, must be regarded as sadism that has been turned around upon the subject's own ego.

But, there is no difference in principle between an instinct turning from an object to the ego and its turning from the ego to an object—which is the novelty now under discussion. Masochism, the turning around of the instinct upon the object's own ego, would appear, in fact, to be a return to an earlier phase of the instinct's history, a regression. The account that was then given of masochism would need to be emended for being too sweeping: there *might* be such a thing as primary masochism—a possibility that I contested at that time.

Let us, however, return to the self-preservative sexual instincts. The experiments upon protista have already shown us that conjugation—that is, the coalescence of two individuals that separate soon afterward, without any subsequent cell-division occurring—has a strengthening and rejuvenating effect upon both of them.

In later generations, they show no signs of degenerating and seem able to put up a longer resistance to the injurious effects of their own metabolism. This single observation may, I think, be taken as typical of the effect produced by sexual union as well. But how is it that the coalescence of two only slightly different cells can bring about this renewal of life?

The experiment, which replaces the conjugation of protozoa by the application of chemical or even of mechanical stimuli (Lipschütz, 1914), enables us to give what is, no doubt, a conclusive reply to this question. The result is brought about by the influx of fresh amounts of stimulus. This tallies well with the hypothesis that the vital process of the individual leads, for internal reasons, to an equalization of chemical tensions—that is to say, to death, whereas union with the living substance of a different individual increases those tensions, introducing what may be described as fresh, vital differences of potential, which must then be lived down.

As regards these differences, there must of course be one or more optima. The dominating tendency of mental life, and perhaps of nervous life in general, is the effort to reduce, to keep constant or to remove internal tension due to stimuli—the Nirvana principle, to borrow a term from Barbara Low—a tendency, which finds expression in the pleasure principle; and our recognition of that fact is one of our strongest reasons for believing in the existence of death instincts.

But, we still feel our line of thought appreciably hampered by the fact that we cannot ascribe to the sexual instinct, the characteristic of a compulsion to repeat, which first put us on the track of the death instincts. The sphere of embryonic developmental processes is, no doubt, extremely rich in such phenomena of repetition. The two germ-cells that are involved in sexual reproduction, and their life history, are, themselves, only repetitions of the beginnings of organic life. But the essence of the processes, to which sexual life is directed, is the coalescence of two cell bodies. That, alone, is what guarantees the immortality of the living substance in the higher organisms.

In other words, we need more information on the origin of sexual reproduction and of the sexual instincts, in general. This is a problem, which is calculated to daunt an outsider, and which the specialists, themselves, have not yet been able to solve. We shall, therefore, give only the briefest summary of whatever seems relevant to our line of thought, from among the many discordant assertions and opinions.

One of these views deprives the problem of reproduction of its mysterious fascination by representing it as a part manifestation of growth. The origin of reproduction by sexually differentiated germ-cells might be pictured along sober Darwinian lines, by supposing that the advantage of amphimixis, arrived at, on some occasion, by the chance conjugation of two protista, was retained and further exploited in later development.

On this view, sex would not be anything very ancient; and the extraordinarily violent instincts, whose aim it is to bring about sexual union, would be repeating something that had once occurred by chance and had, since, become established as being advantageous.

The question arises here, as in the case of death, whether we are only justified in ascribing to the protista those characteristics they actually exhibit, and whether it is right to assume that forces and processes that only become visible in the higher organisms, first originated in those organisms.

The view of sexuality we have just mentioned is of little help for our purposes. The objection may be raised against it that it postulates the existence of life instincts already operating in the simplest organisms; for otherwise conjugation, which works counter to the course of life and makes the task of ceasing to live more difficult, would not be retained and elaborated, but would be avoided.

If, therefore, we are not to abandon the hypothesis of death instincts, we must suppose them to be associated from the very first with life instincts. But, it must be admitted that, in that case, we shall be working upon an equation with two unknown quantities.

Apart from this, science has so little to tell us about the origin of sexuality that we can liken the problem to a darkness, into which, not so much as a ray of an hypothesis has penetrated. In quite a different region, it is true, we *do* meet with such an hypothesis; but it is of so fantastic a kind—a myth rather than a scientific explanation—that I should not venture to produce it here, were it not that it fulfills precisely the one condition whose fulfillment we desire. For it traces the origin of an instinct to a need to restore an earlier state of things.

What I have in mind is, of course, the theory that Plato put into the mouth of Aristophanes in the *Symposium*, and which deals not only with the origin of the sexual instinct, but also with the most important of its variations in relation to its object:

"The original human nature was not like the present, but different. In the first place, the sexes were originally three in number, not two as they are now; there was man, woman, and the union of the two..."

Everything about these primeval men was double: they had four hands and four feet, two faces, two privy parts, and so on. Eventually, Zeus decided to cut these men in two, "like a sorb-apple which is halved for pickling."

After the division had been made, "the two parts of man, each desiring his other half, came together, and threw their arms about one another eager to grow into one."

Shall we follow the hint given us by the poet philosopher, and venture upon the hypothesis that living substance, at the time of its coming to life, was torn apart into small particles, which have ever since endeavored to reunite through the sexual instincts? that these instincts, in which the chemical affinity of inanimate matter persisted, gradually succeeded, as they developed through the kingdom of the protista, in overcoming the difficulties put in the way of that endeavor, by an environment charged with dangerous stimuli—stimuli which compelled them to form a protective cortical layer? that these splintered fragments of living substance, in this way, attained a multi-cellular condition and finally transferred the instinct for reuniting, in the most highly concentrated form, to the germ-cells?

But here, I think, the moment has come for breaking off. Not, however, without the addition of a few words of critical reflection. It may be asked whether, and how far, I am, myself, convinced of the truth of the hypotheses that have been set out in these pages. My answer would be that I am not convinced, myself, and that I do not seek to persuade other people to believe in them.

Or, more precisely, that I do not know how far I believe in them. There is no reason, as it seems to me, why the emotional factor of conviction should enter into this question at all. It is surely possible to throw oneself into a line of thought and to follow it wherever it leads, out of simple scientific curiosity, or, if the reader prefers, as an *advocatus diaboli*, who is not on that account himself sold to the devil.

I do not dispute the fact that the third step in the theory of the instincts, which I have taken here, cannot lay claim to the same degree of certainty as the two earlier ones—the extension of the concept of sexuality and the hypothesis of narcissism. These two innovations were a direct translation of observation into theory and were no more open to sources of error than is inevitable in all such cases.

It is true that my assertion of the regressive character of instincts also rests upon observed material—namely on the facts of the compulsion to repeat. It may be, however, that I have overestimated their significance, and, in any case, it is impossible to pursue an idea of this kind except by repeatedly combining factual material with what is purely speculative, and, thus, diverging widely from observation.

The more frequently this is done in the course of constructing a theory, the more untrustworthy, as we know, must be the final result. But, the degree of uncertainty is not assignable. One may have made a lucky hit or one may have gone shamefully astray. I do not attach much importance to the part played by what is called intuition in work of this kind.

What I have seen of it, seems to me, rather, to be the result of a kind of intellectual impartiality. Unfortunately, however, people are seldom impartial where ultimate things, the great problems of science and life, are concerned. Each of us is governed, in such cases, by deep-rooted internal prejudices, into whose hands our speculation unwittingly plays. Because we have such good grounds for being distrustful, our attitude toward the results of our own deliberations cannot well be other than one of cool benevolence.

I hasten to add, however, that self-criticism such as this is far from binding one to any special tolerance toward dissentient opinions. It is perfectly legitimate to reject, remorselessly, theories that are contradicted by the very first steps in the analysis of observed facts, while yet being aware, at the same time, that the validity of one's own theory is only a provisional one.

We need not feel greatly disturbed in judging our speculation upon the life and death instincts by the fact that so many bewildering and obscure processes occur in it—such as one instinct being driven out by another or an instinct turning from the ego to an object, and so on. This is merely due to our being obliged to operate with scientific terms, that is to say with the figurative language peculiar to psychology (or, more precisely, to depth psychology).

We could not otherwise describe the processes in question at all, and indeed, we could not have become aware of them. The deficiencies in our description would probably vanish if we were already in a position to replace the psychological terms by physiological or chemical ones. It is true that they, too, are only part of a figurative language; but it is one with which we have long been familiar, and which is, perhaps, a simpler one as well.

On the other hand, it should be made quite clear that the uncertainty of our speculation has been greatly increased by the necessity for borrowing from the science of biology. Biology is truly a land of unlimited possibilities. We may expect it to give us the most surprising information, and we cannot guess what answers it will return in a few dozen years to the questions we have put to it.

They may be of a kind that will blow away the whole of our artificial structure of hypotheses. If so, it may be asked, why I have embarked upon such a line of thought as the present one, and in particular, why I have decided to make it public. Well—I cannot deny that some of the analogies, correlations, and connections that it contains seemed to me to deserve consideration.

I will add a few words to clarify our terminology, which has undergone some development in the course of the present work. We came to know what the sexual instincts were, from their relation to the sexes and to the reproductive function. We retained this name after we had been obliged by the findings of psychoanalysis, to connect them less closely with reproduction. With the hypothesis of narcissistic libido, and the extension of the concept of libido to the individual cells, the sexual instinct was transformed for us into Eros, which seeks to force together and hold together the portions of living substance.

What are commonly called the sexual instincts are looked upon, by us, as the part of Eros that is directed towards objects. Our speculations have suggested that Eros operates from the beginning of life and appears as a life instinct, in opposition to the death instinct, which was brought into being by the coming to life of inorganic substance.

These speculations seek to solve the riddle of life by supposing that these two instincts were struggling with each other from the very first. It is not so easy, perhaps, to follow the transformations through which the concept of the ego instincts has passed. To begin with, we applied that name to all the instinctual trends (of which we had no closer knowledge), which could be distinguished from the sexual instincts directed towards an object. We opposed the ego instincts to the sexual instincts of which the libido is the manifestation.

Subsequently, we came to closer grips with the analysis of the ego and recognized that a portion of the ego instincts is also of a libidinal character and has taken the subject's own ego as its object. These narcissistic self-preservative instincts had thenceforward to be counted among the libidinal sexual instincts.

The opposition between the ego instincts and the sexual instincts was transformed into one, between the ego instincts and the object instincts, both of a libidinal nature. But, in its place, a fresh opposition appeared between the libidinal (ego and object) instincts and others, which must be presumed to be present in the ego and which may actually be observed in the destructive instincts.

Our speculations have transformed this opposition into one between the life instincts (Eros) and the death instincts.

Chapter Seven

If it is really the case, that seeking to restore an earlier state of things is such a universal characteristic of instincts, we need not be surprised that so many processes take place in mental life independently of the pleasure principle. This characteristic would be shared by all the component instincts, and, in their case, would aim at returning once more to a particular stage in the course of development.

These are matters over which the pleasure principle has, as yet, no control; but it does not follow that any of them are necessarily opposed to it, and we have still to solve the problem of the relation of the instinctual processes of repetition to the dominance of the pleasure principle.

We have found that one of the earliest and most important functions of the mental apparatus is to bind the instinctual impulses which impinge on it, to replace the primary process prevailing in them, by the secondary process and to convert their mobile cathectic energy into a predominantly quiescent (tonic) cathexis.

While this transformation is taking place, no attention can be paid to the development of unpleasure; but this does not imply the suspension of the pleasure principle. On the contrary, the transformation occurs in the service of the pleasure principle; the binding is a preparatory act that introduces and assures the dominance of the pleasure principle.

Let us make a sharper distinction than we have so far made between function and tendency. The pleasure principle, then, is a tendency operating in the service of a function, whose business it is to free the mental apparatus entirely from excitation, or to keep the amount of excitation in it constant, or to keep it as low as possible.

We cannot yet decide with certainty in favor of any of these ways of putting it; but it is clear that the function thus described would be concerned with the most universal endeavor of all living substance—namely, to return to the quiescence of the inorganic world. We have all experienced how the greatest pleasure attainable, that of the sexual act, is associated with a momentary extinction of a highly intensified excitation.

The binding of an instinctual impulse would be a preliminary function designed to prepare the excitation for its final elimination in the pleasure of discharge.

This raises the question of whether feelings of pleasure and unpleasure can be produced equally from bound and from unbound excitational processes. And, there seems to be no doubt, what-so-ever, that the unbound or primary processes give rise to far more intense feelings, in both directions, than the bound or secondary ones. Moreover, the primary processes are the earlier in time; at the beginning of mental life, there are no others, and we may infer that if the pleasure principle had not already been operative in *them,* it could never have been established for the later ones.

We thus reach what is at bottom, no very simple conclusion, namely that at the beginning of mental life, the struggle for pleasure was far more intense than later, but not so unrestricted. It had to submit to frequent interruptions. In later times, the dominance of the pleasure principle is very much more secure, but it, itself, has no more escaped the process of taming than the other instincts in general. In any case, whatever it is that causes the appearance of feelings of pleasure and unpleasure, in processes of excitation, must be present in the secondary process, just as it is in the primary one.

Here might be the starting-point for fresh investigations. Our consciousness communicates to us feelings from within, not only of pleasure and unpleasure, but also of a peculiar tension, which, in its turn, can be either pleasurable or unpleasurable. Should the difference between these feelings enable us to distinguish between bound and unbound processes of energy? or is the feeling of tension to be related to the absolute magnitude, or perhaps to the level, of the cathexis, while the pleasure and unpleasure series indicates a change in the magnitude of the cathexis *within a given unit of time?*

Another striking fact is that the life instincts have so much more contact with our internal perception—emerging as breakers of the peace and constantly producing tensions, whose release is felt as pleasure—while the death instincts seem to do their work unobtrusively. The pleasure principle seems actually to serve the death instincts.

It is true that it keeps watch upon stimuli from without, which are regarded as dangers by both kinds of instincts. It is more especially on guard against increases of stimulation from within, which would make the task of living more difficult.

This, in turn, raises a host of other questions to which we can, at present, find no answer. We must be patient and await fresh methods and occasions of research. We must be ready, too, to abandon a path that we have followed for a time, if it seems to be leading to no good end.

Only believers, who demand that science shall be a substitute for the catechism they have given up, will blame an investigator for developing or even transforming his views. We may take comfort, too, for the slow advances of our scientific knowledge in the words of the poet:

Was man nicht erfliegen kann, muss man erhinken. (What we cannot reach flying, we must reach limping.)